Animal Helpers for the Disabled

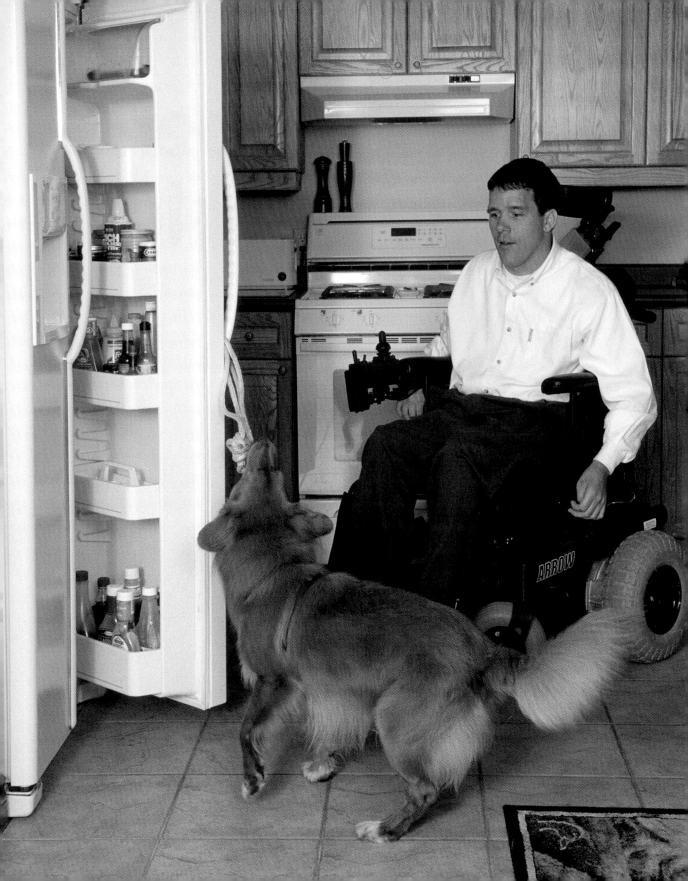

Animal Helpers for the Disabled

Deborah Kent

Franklin Watts
A Division of Scholastic Inc.
New York • Toronto • London • Auckland • Sydney
Mexico City • New Delhi • Hong Kong
Danbury, Connecticut

Note to readers: Definitions for words in **bold** can be found in the Glossary at the back of this book.

Photographs © 2002: AP/Wide World Photos: 48 (Ron Berard), 22 (Miranda Meyer), 29 (Steven Senne), 8; Canine Companions for Independence: 36; Corbis Images: 19 (Bettmann), 17 (Catherine Karnow), 32, 43, 46 (Tom Nebbia), 25 (Bob Rowan), 33 (David H. Wells), 11; International Hearing Dog Inc.: 21, 24; Photo Researchers, NY: 2 (Carolyn A. McKeone), 39 (Lawrence Migdale); PhotoEdit: cover, 51 (Stephen McBrady), 26 (Mark Richards), 28 (Robin L. Sachs), 14, 34 (Frank Siteman); Stock Boston/Frank Siteman: 31, 35; The Seeing Eye: 6, 9, 41; Woodfin Camp & Associates/A. Ramey: 12.

The photograph on the cover shows a young woman walking on a sidewalk with her dog guide. The photograph opposite the title page shows an assistance dog opening a refrigerator for its owner.

Library of Congress Cataloging-in-Publication Data

Kent, Deborah.
    Animal helpers for the disabled / by Deborah Kent.
        p. cm. — (Watts library)
    Summary: Explores the history of guide dogs, service animals, and assistance dogs, and discusses the process of training them to help who have physical disabilities.
    Includes bibliographical references and index.
    ISBN 0-531-12017-1 (lib. bdg.)   0-531-16663-5 (pbk.)
    1. Animals as aids for people with disabilities—Juvenile literature. [1. Animals—Therapeutic use. 2. Working animals. 3. Animals—Training. 4. Guide dogs. 5. Dogs.] I. Title. II. Series.
HV1569.6.K46 2003
636.088'6—dc21   2002008885

Contents

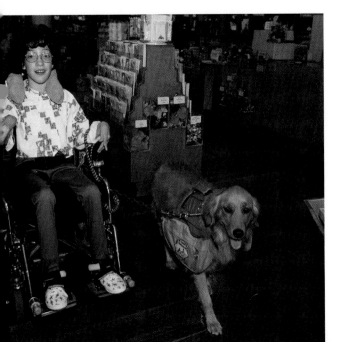

Morris Frank traveled from the United States to Switzerland to obtain a dog guide. He hoped that the dog guide would enable him to be more independent.

Chapter One

"Buddy, Forward!"

When twenty-year-old Morris Frank sailed to Europe in 1928, the ship's steward locked him into his cabin at night. By day an escort led Frank to and from the dining room for meals. Morris Frank was not a convict, crossing the Atlantic under guard. He was subjected to this humiliating treatment to keep him out of harm's way—only because he was blind.

In spite of the steward, Frank was filled with excitement. He had begun the adventure of a lifetime. A year before,

Dorothy Harrison Eustis sits with two of her dog guides. Her efforts helped many blind people.

Frank listened enthralled as his father read him an article from the popular magazine *The Saturday Evening Post*. The author, Dorothy Harrison Eustis, described a program in Potsdam, Germany, that trained dogs to guide blinded veterans of World War I. Such a dog could lead its master around obstacles and warn him of curbs and stairways. Eustis had visited the Potsdam school and was highly impressed. Born in the United States, Eustis had been training police dogs and rescue dogs on her estate in Switzerland. Now she hoped to train dog guides there.

Morris Frank wrote to Eustis immediately. "Is what you say really true?" he asked. "If so, I want one of those dogs! And I am not alone. Thousands of blind people, like me, abhor being dependent on others. Help me and I will help them. Train me, and I will bring back my dog and show people here how a blind man can be absolutely on his own." After an exchange of letters, telegrams, and phone calls, everything was arranged. Morris Frank would be the first blind student in Eustis's pilot program.

After his ship docked in Paris, Frank took a train to the town of Vevey in the Swiss Alps. There he met Eustis, who drove him to her nearby estate, Fortunate Fields. The day after Frank arrived, trainer Jack Humphrey introduced him to his new dog. She was a beautiful German shepherd with an improbable name—Kiss. Later Frank described his first reaction: "'Kiss!' I exclaimed. My face turned red as I pictured my embarrassment at calling out, 'Here, Kiss! Come, Kiss!' in a crowd of strangers. 'That's a hell of a name for a dog,' I [said] brusquely. Then I put my arms around my new friend and told her, 'I'm going to call you Buddy.'"

For the next several weeks Humphrey taught Frank to follow Buddy's signals. While at work, Buddy wore a sturdy leather harness. By holding the harness's U-shaped handle, Frank could read the dog's subtlest movements. He learned to follow

Morris Frank walks with Buddy through the streets of Vevey, Switzerland.

closely as Buddy steered him around baby carriages, sidewalk vending stands, and open manholes. Buddy slowed down when they walked through crowds, and came to a complete stop to indicate a curb or set of stairs.

In order to work with Buddy effectively, Frank had to give her clear, crisp commands. When he picked up the harness handle to start off on a walk he commanded, "Buddy, forward!" When he wanted to turn a corner, he ordered, "Buddy, right!" or "Buddy, left!" Buddy helped him avoid obstacles in his path, but he had to say which way he wanted to go.

Sometimes Frank grew discouraged. He misread Buddy's signals or gave weak commands that failed to catch Buddy's attention. But little by little the young man and the beautiful gray German shepherd became a working team. The breakthrough came one day when Frank decided he needed a haircut. In the past he had to wait for someone to take him to and from the barbershop. Now he and Buddy set out alone. Frank returned to Fortunate Fields later that day with a new haircut and an exhilarating new sense of freedom.

Keeping a Promise

Just as he promised in his letter to Dorothy Eustis, Frank was eager to spread the dog-guide movement to the United States. When he and Buddy completed their training in Switzerland, they returned to Frank's home in Nashville, Tennessee. A team of Swiss-trained instructors soon followed. Eustis poured her efforts into fund-raising. In 1929 the new school

opened in Nashville, training five blind students to work with **dog guides**. In 1931 the school moved to spacious quarters in Morristown, New Jersey. The school needed a name, and the staff decided to call it The Seeing Eye.

The Seeing Eye was the first school in the United States to train dogs to help people with disabilities. In the decades that followed, several other dog-guide schools opened their doors. Then, in the 1980s, people with disabilities other than

An instructor works with two students on crossing the street with their Seeing Eye dogs.

A young woman with disabilities visits a store with her companion dog.

blindness became interested in the help that specially trained dogs could provide. Today, a number of programs train **hearing dogs** for deaf people and service dogs for people with

limited mobility. A hearing, or signal, dog alerts a deaf person to such sounds as a knock at the door, a smoke alarm, or a crying baby. Service dogs pick up dropped objects, press light switches, and open doors.

From Australia to Norway, from Japan to South Africa, men and women with disabilities share their lives with canine partners. In each partnership, dog and human depend on one another and work together as a team. Morris Frank launched a worldwide movement the first time he uttered the fateful words, "Buddy, forward!"

Getting It Straight

There are many terms used to describe animals that help people with disabilities, and the language can be confusing. The term service animal refers to any animal trained to help a person with a disability. Most service animals are dogs, but some trained monkeys and horses also fit this description. The term **assistance dog** includes guide dogs for the blind, hearing dogs for the deaf, and service dogs for the physically disabled.

Signal, or hearing, dogs help their owners by alerting them to sounds, such as a telephone ringing or a baby crying.

Chapter Two

Working Together

Seeing a working dog like Chelsea [is] a moving experience. The work relationship gave a dimension to ... dog/human interaction that few people ... have the chance to observe .... It ... came to me [while with Chelsea] how hard it would be to receive from a human being the help [Chelsea] gave me so freely and eagerly.

—Paul Ogden, from *Chelsea: The Story of a Signal Dog*

Bridging the Chasm

It has often been said that the dog is man's best friend. Since prehistoric times dogs have lived among human beings, and both species have benefited from the connection. Dogs lived with nomadic tribes of hunters and gatherers. They barked to warn of approaching enemies and in return received food and shelter from their human companions. When humans turned to farming, dogs guarded their herds from wolves and other predators. Later, humans became city dwellers. Dogs were still with them, offering protection and loyalty in return for the care only a human master could provide.

As long as there have been humans on Earth, there have been people with disabilities. In every culture, at every period in history, some people are born deaf or blind or with limited movement. Others become disabled due to illness or injury. Warfare has always been with us, and a by-product of war has always been disabling injuries. From the beginning, then, dogs and disabled people have almost surely been in contact with one another. Since humans are endlessly resourceful, and since dogs are intelligent, teachable, and eager to please, it stands to reason that some disabled people trained dogs to help them, even in the remotest past.

Historical records of assistance dogs are sparse, but medieval paintings show blind beggars accompanied by dogs, who apparently served as guides and protectors. Most dogs have an uncanny memory for places they have visited, as though they carry a kind of mental map of their surroundings.

A blind person with a dog might readily put this ability to good use. By resting a hand on the dog's back or holding onto a leash or makeshift harness, he or she could follow the dog through crowded city streets to a familiar destination.

Deaf persons, too, have long made use of canine talents. Dogs naturally alert their owners to a knock on the door by barking. A deaf person could train his dog to alert him in a different way, by nuzzling him or tugging him toward the door. In his 1872 novel *Smoke*, the Russian writer Ivan Turgenev described the relationship between a deaf peasant and his dog. When strangers approached the dog let his

For centuries, dogs have played an important role in farming and raising livestock.

17

master know by thrusting its muzzle into its master's hand and pawing at his legs.

After World War I, a new concept took hold in Europe and the United States, the idea that disabled veterans could be retrained to take their place in society. In Germany the thrust for **rehabilitation** led the government to establish four schools for the training of dogs to guide blinded veterans.

The Growth of the Movement

When The Seeing Eye opened, first in Nashville and later in Morristown, the school modeled itself on the program Dorothy Eustis observed in Germany. Nearly all of the dogs used were female German shepherds—males were thought to be too aggressive and hard to handle. Like the Potsdam dogs, dogs at The Seeing Eye learned to stop at intersections and to steer a human partner around obstructions. Gradually, new commands and standards began to evolve. For instance, the American dogs were directed to stand still at a flight of stairs, not to sit down as the dogs in Germany were taught.

Morris Frank and Buddy show the people of New York City how dog guides can lead people who are blind through busy sidewalks and traffic.

During the 1930s Morris Frank and Buddy traveled throughout the United States, recruiting blind students and informing the public about the abilities of blind people paired with well-trained dog guides. The program gained a high profile in the media. People were moved by stories of devoted dogs and determined blind men and women. Donations poured in, and The Seeing Eye flourished.

To meet the growing demand, more dog-guide schools were established. Leader Dogs for the Blind, sponsored by Lions International, was founded in Rochester, Michigan, in 1938. Today fourteen schools in the United States train guide dogs, including Pilot Dogs, in Columbus, Ohio; Guiding Eyes for the Blind, in Yorktown Heights, New York; and Guide Dogs for the Blind, in San Rafael, California. Japan, Australia, Israel, South Africa, Russia, England, and most of the countries in western Europe all have dog-guide programs.

Initially, dog-guide schools obtained dogs in several ways. Some were purchased, and others were donated by breeders or interested individuals. By the 1970s, The Seeing Eye and other schools started to breed their own dogs, selecting for intelligence, stamina, and temperament. Golden retrievers and Labrador retrievers are widely used today, in addition to German shepherds.

In 1975 a trainer named Agnes McGrath explored the idea of training dogs to assist deaf people. She trained six hearing dogs, with the support of the Minnesota Society for the Prevention of Cruelty to Animals (SPCA). Her success led to the founding of a full-scale training program in Denver, Colorado.

In 1979 Paws with a Cause, a program based in Byron Center, Michigan, began training both hearing and service

What's in a Name?

Because The Seeing Eye is so well known, many people refer to all dog guides as "Seeing Eye dogs." Actually this term only applies to dogs trained at the school in Morristown. Each dog guide school uses a slightly different harness and leash to help distinguish its dogs from others.

dogs. During the 1980s similar programs sprang up across the country. In 1993 a group of men and women who use assistance dogs gathered in St. Louis, Missouri, to found the International Association of Assistance Dog Partners (IAADP). The organization encourages people partnered with dog guides, hearing dogs, and service dogs to work together on shared concerns.

Agnes McGrath poses with Candy, the first hearing dog placed by the International Hearing Dog, Inc. McGrath helped found this organization in 1979.

Sherry Caramazza instructs her assistance dog Chris to sit by pointing a finger to her cheek.

In general, the public greatly admires assistance dogs. Their accomplishments are often seen as heroic, even miraculous. Yet assistance dogs have not always been welcome in restaurants, theaters, schools, or other public places. Even today assistance-dog users sometimes encounter barriers based on ignorance, prejudice, and fear.

Laying Down the Law

During the early years of The Seeing Eye, Morris Frank and other dog-guide users heard one dreaded phrase over and over again: "No dogs allowed!" All too often they were turned away from restaurants, ordered out of stores, and banned from churches and classrooms when they tried to enter with their dog guides. These early handlers became ambassadors of goodwill for the assistance-dog movement. Step-by-step, on a case-by-case basis, they persuaded the public that a well-trained working dog would cause no trouble to anyone. The strongest evidence was the behavior of the dogs themselves. When people saw that dog guides were quiet, clean, and under the owner's control, barriers began to crumble.

All Aboard!

In the early 1930s railroad officials required dog guides to be crated and carried in a baggage car. The tireless efforts of Morris Frank, Dorothy Eustis, and others persuaded the railroads to change their policy. By 1935 all U.S. railroad companies allowed guide dogs to ride with their owners in passenger cars.

Many laws were passed to allow animal helpers to accompany their owners to public places.

White Cane Laws

The laws that cover dog guides are generally known as white cane laws, because they cover all blind people, including those who travel with the use of the long white cane.

Over the years one state after another passed laws ensuring blind people full access to public accommodations when accompanied by dog guides. In the 1980s these laws were expanded to cover persons with hearing and service dogs as well.

In 1990 the U.S. Congress passed the landmark **legislation** known as the **Americans with Disabilities Act** (ADA). The ADA grants disabled Americans the right to be accompanied by service animals in all places of public accommodation. In

order to qualify under the law, the animal must be trained to perform specific tasks that assist the disabled person. In addition, it must be well behaved and under the owner's control.

Despite federal, state, and local laws guaranteeing access to assistance dogs, problems still occasionally arise. Now and then a taxi driver or a landlord refuses to accept a person with an assistance dog. Such incidents are painful and humiliating to the dog's owner. The effort to educate the public, begun by Morris Frank in the 1930s, goes on in the twenty-first century.

An office worker takes her dog guide to her job. The Americans with Disabilities Act allows some service animals to go to work with their owners.

A person who is blind and his dog guide work together, helping the person reach his destination.

Chapter Three

Partners for Independence

*All through the first walk, the physical activity,
the mental preoccupation, the warmth of grati-
tude, the sense of novelty and independence
possessed me entirely, and I lost track of the
number of blocks and turns on the quiet street,
feeling quite alone with myself and Minnie.*

—Peter Putnam, from
Keep Your Head Up, Mr. Putnam

Navigating the World

A person who is blind and wants to travel
independently has two options. She can

A young woman, who is blind, uses a white cane to help her get to her classes at school.

use a long white cane or she can work with a guide dog. Both travel methods are effective, and both have advantages and drawbacks. By tapping the cane in a low arc in front of her, the blind person can detect steps, poles, and other obstacles in time to avoid bumping into them or tripping. If she chooses partnership with a dog guide, the dog will indicate obstacles to her, or simply skirt around them without breaking their pace.

In order to guide its human partner around an abandoned tricycle or other object in their path, the dog guide must judge

Get a Horse!

In 2000 the North Carolina-based Guide Horse Foundation began training miniature horses to guide blind people. About the size of a large dog, the miniature horse is friendly and intelligent. The working life of a guide horse can range from twenty to thirty years, considerably longer than eight to ten years for a dog guide. However, a guide horse is clearly not for everyone. Horses may be at home on the range, but not in a high-rise apartment building or on a 747 airplane. The guide horse and its human partner need a thoroughly rural lifestyle. Dan Shaw, a blind farmer from Maine, obtained the first guide horse in 2001.

the extra width of the human at its side. It must provide enough **clearance** so that the blind person can pass the obstacle without grazing it. Dog guides must also learn to watch out for low-hanging branches or awnings at human head or shoulder height.

People sometimes think that a blind person says, "Take me to the supermarket," and lets the dog do the rest. In reality, dog and human work as a team to get from one place to another. The blind person must know where he or she is going and must give the dog step-by-step instructions. These instructions are based on three simple commands: "left," "right," and "forward." Street crossings require especially careful teamwork. The dog stops at the curb. The human listens to the flow of traffic to gauge whether she has the light. When she believes it is safe to cross she gives the forward command. But if the dog sees a car coming, it refuses to enter the street. Thus the dog overrides the command if it feels that the situation is unsafe. Dog-guide trainers refer to this decision-making ability as **intelligent disobedience**.

Signals and Warnings

A person who is deaf relies upon sight as his primary source of information. In his home he may set up lights that flash on when the doorbell rings or the dinner in the microwave is heated. But not every room can be rigged with these lighting devices, and lights cannot warn of every sound that may prove important. Hearing dogs are trained to alert deaf persons to such sounds as a knock, a ringing doorbell, a crying baby, an oven timer, an alarm clock, or any unusual noise that ought to be investigated. One man described how his hearing dog led him to a kitchen cupboard, where he discovered a mouse gnawing on a piece of bread.

A hearing dog alerts its owner that the alarm clock is ringing.

Hearing dogs are also trained to alert their human partners to sounds outdoors. At the wailing of a siren or the warning honk of a car horn, the dog sits down abruptly or steps in front of its owner to block his way. One of the dog's most crucial tasks is to let its partner know if someone is trying to get his attention. If someone calls to the deaf person from behind or off to the side, out of his line of vision, the dog alerts him by touching him with a paw. Then it points its muzzle toward the person who called.

Hearing dogs come in all shapes and sizes. Small breeds such as corgis, spaniels, and terriers are often used, as well as dogs of mixed breeds.

The Yellow Leash

For identification, hearing dogs usually wear a distinctive orange or yellow leash emblazoned with the name of the school where the dog was trained.

31

Nose, Paws, and Power

The service-dog movement, which gathered momentum in the 1990s, makes creative use of all of the dog's strengths and abilities. The needs and capacities of physically disabled persons vary tremendously, and each service-dog user works with his dog in different ways.

For people with limited hand use, a service dog can switch lights on with the flick of a paw. Nudging with its nose, it can

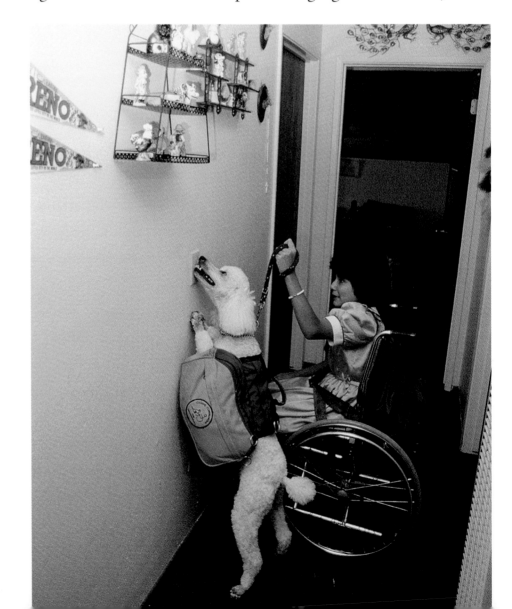

A service dog turns on the light for a girl in a wheelchair.

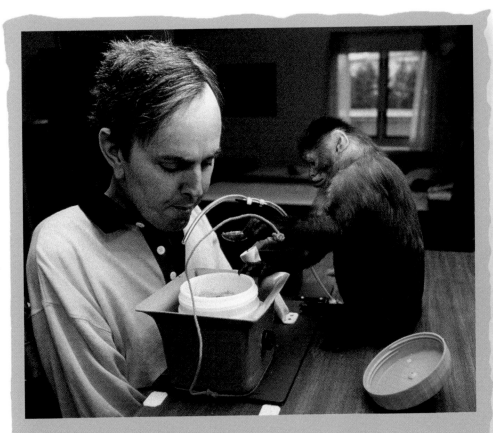

Helping Hands

The Helping Hands Foundation in Boston, Massachusetts, trains capuchin monkeys to perform tasks for people with severe physical disabilities. Monkeys learn quickly, and their humanlike hands are well designed to push buttons, open drawers, and carry small objects. But the monkey temperament—high-strung and independent—can make these partnerships a real challenge. From a practical standpoint monkeys have serious limitations as service animals.

open a cupboard door. Once the door is open the dog can fetch whatever box or can his human partner desires. Service dogs can pick up dropped objects and, stretching on hind legs, even deliver money to a salesperson at a counter.

Putting Fear Aside

Therapy dogs are used in the treatment of psychiatric patients, especially children who are emotionally disturbed. The love of a gentle dog can provide healing comfort to a child traumatized by abuse.

Like dog guides, most service dogs are relatively large. Many breeds are used, including German shepherds, golden retrievers, and Samoyeds. A service dog can lend its strength to a person with disabilities by pulling a wheelchair or carrying a small backpack. For a person whose balance is uncertain when walking, a dog can be trained to provide physical support. The dog wears a harness that the human partner holds, gaining extra support from the dog's four legs.

The Healing Power of Love

Studies show that people who have pets live longer and happier lives than people without them. As early as the 1970s, some nursing homes regularly brought in dogs to visit the residents. By the 1990s trained **companion dogs** were being used in nursing homes and hospitals throughout the United States.

Companion dogs enrich the lives of thousands of people each year. For a sick child or an elderly woman with Alzheimer's disease, a dog's soft coat and wagging tail sometimes have almost magical powers. Companion dogs are

trained to remain calm and steady, to stand quietly while they are petted and fussed over. A companion dog must be very tolerant of handling by an ever-changing array of people. Its work is to be lovable and loving.

Unlike dog guides and hearing and service dogs, companion dogs do not perform specific tasks for disabled persons. They are not considered assistance dogs under the law. Companion dogs are essentially pets, though they are pets with a purpose.

An elderly man holds a companion dog. While they are not trained to open doors or help someone walk across the street, these dogs provide love and support to the people they visit.

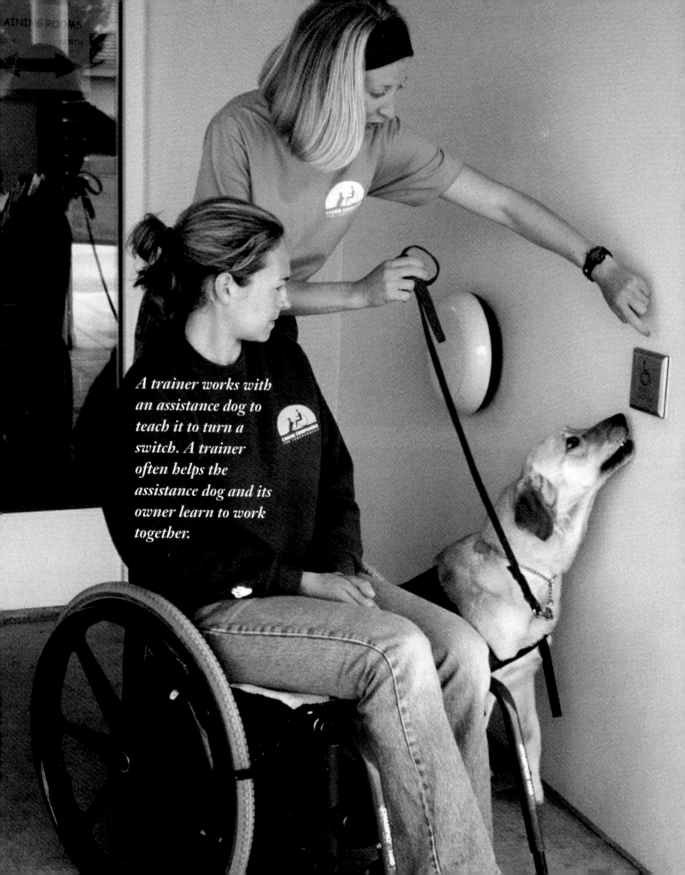

A trainer works with an assistance dog to teach it to turn a switch. A trainer often helps the assistance dog and its owner learn to work together.

Chapter Four

Going to School

For me, the most rewarding part of my work as a trainer is seeing the dogs enrich the lives of those with whom they are placed and seeing how the dogs respond by surpassing our expectations.

—Paul Mundell, a trainer with
Canine Companions for Independence,
Santa Rosa, California

Learning the Basics

Assistance dogs ride in taxis, go to restaurants, and cruise through shopping malls.

They attend concerts, plays, movies, and church services. In national parks and theme parks, classrooms and courtrooms they come and go freely with their human partners. Assistance dogs have rights and privileges not accorded to other dogs, and they have to earn these rights by impeccable behavior. Before a dog masters the special tasks of assistance work, it needs to learn the basics of good canine manners.

While they are puppies, most future dog guides are placed with families that live near the dog-guide school. The family raises the puppy until it is fourteen to eighteen months old. During this critical period the dog learns how to behave in a busy household—to stay off the furniture, to leave the garbage pail alone, to keep its nose off the kitchen counters. It gets used to the roar of a vacuum cleaner, the slamming of doors, and all the other noises of family life.

In addition, puppy raisers introduce the dog to an array of experiences outside the home. They take it for walks along busy streets where it sees and hears traffic. They bring it into crowded stores, take it up and down elevators, and lead it on board buses and trains. Many of these situations will be part of the dog's work as a guide later on.

Generally hearing- and service-dog programs acquire their dogs when they are past the puppy stage. Many dogs are donated and some are recruited from animal shelters. These dogs, with their widely varied backgrounds, must be carefully screened before they enter training.

Head, Heart, Hands, and Health

The motto of the 4-H Club, an organization for girls and boys, is "Learning through Doing." In many parts of the United States children in the 4-H Club raise puppies for dog-guide programs.

A future assistance dog goes to a class as a part of its training.

Preparing to Serve

Formal training for an assistance dog lasts three to four months. A trainer works with the dog for approximately an hour each day. First the trainer works on basic obedience commands such as "come," "fetch," "sit," "down," and "stay." Then the training moves to the specific commands required by a dog guide, hearing dog, or service dog.

Every assistance dog must be an enthusiastic worker, eager to obey the commands of its human partner. Yet each type of assistance work calls for a particular canine personality. A hearing dog must have a high awareness of sound and the ability to respond to specific sounds in a noisy environment. A service dog, however, must be willing to carry out repetitive commands when necessary. For instance, if the dog's owner drops a handful of bills, the dog must pick them up carefully one by one. Not all dogs are able to work in this way. Many lose interest when asked to perform the same task again and again.

Because they make constant decisions in their work, dog guides must possess a confident, independent spirit. If it hears

the forward command yet sees that the sidewalk is blocked by sawhorses, the dog must make a choice. It can approach the barricade and stand still, waiting for its owner to examine the sawhorses and give a new command. Or the dog can decide to steer its partner around the sawhorses. It can turn left and hug the buildings along the sidewalk or turn right and step into the street. Not all dogs have the temperament to act independently in this way.

Most animal trainers rely on a system of rewards and punishments. Food rewards, such as small dog biscuits, are often used in training service dogs and hearing dogs. As training progresses, the food rewards are phased out and the dog learns to work for the praise of its trainer or partner. Some dog-guide trainers are also beginning to experiment with food rewards. But traditionally dog guides have been trained to work solely for praise. An enthusiastic "That's a good girl!" and a pat on the head keep the dog happy and alert.

Becoming a Team

At most assistance-dog programs the staff tries hard to select the dog that will best fit each student's needs and personality. A very active dog that hungers for novelty would be a poor match for a timid young man with a sedentary job at a bank. The banker might be happier with a quiet dog that enjoys a

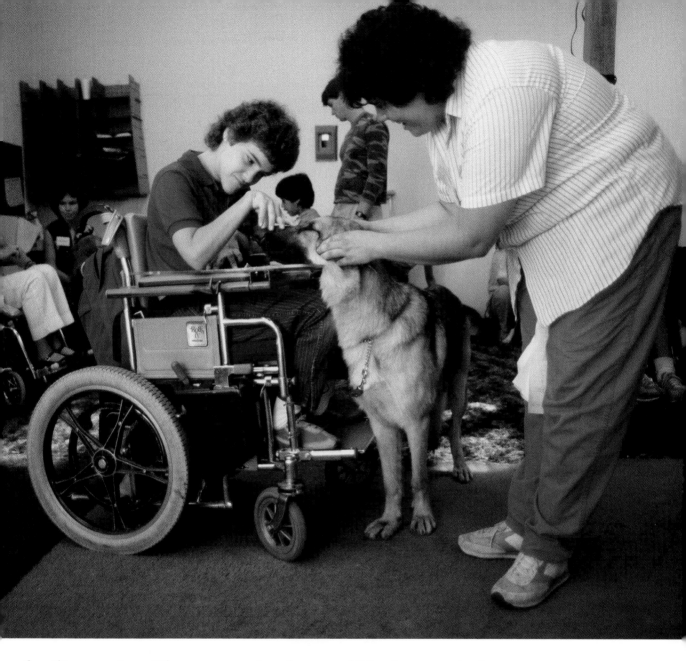

familiar routine. The more active dog would be better suited to life with an outgoing partner who loves to travel.

The first meeting between canine and human partners is a moment of high drama. At many schools the trainer brings the dog to the student's room. The student sits on the floor,

A teenage boy meets a German shepherd that has been trained to assist him.

How Old Do I Have to Be?

Since working with an assistance dog requires maturity, schools prefer a student to be at least sixteen years old. Service and hearing dog programs are somewhat more flexible, and a few dogs have been paired with children as young as seven.

petting and playing with the dog that will be so important in her life. Dog and human begin to form a crucial bond.

In general, students live at an assistance-dog school during their training period. Students paired with hearing or service dogs train for one to two weeks. Students training with dog guides stay at the school for a longer period, from three weeks to a month. A few programs send an instructor to train the student in her own home. But most schools believe that students focus more fully on the training process in a school setting, where they are free from work and family responsibilities.

When dog and student meet, the dog has already completed its training. The human is the one who needs to learn skills and build confidence. Trainers teach the student to give

"Don't Bother Me, I'm Working!"

When an assistance dog is on duty, it must not be distracted by petting and playing. If the dog is distracted, it will not work effectively, and the team could even be at risk of injury. Some dogs wear a sign announcing that they are at work.

commands and to reward good behavior. The student also learns to correct the dog if it misbehaves.

Training takes student and dog into a variety of situations they are likely to encounter back home. They eat in restaurants, ride buses and subways, and explore shopping malls. Dog-guide users practice crossing busy streets and walking on roads without sidewalks. In addition, students attend lectures about feeding, grooming, and maintaining the dog's health. They learn about legislation covering access for assistance dogs.

By the time they leave the school, student and assistance dog have become a team. In the years to come, they will share triumphs and frustrations, moving through the world together, as partners.

Andrew Cosell, who has cerebral palsy, receives some affection from his assistance dog. His dog helps him with tasks in his daily life.

Chapter Five

Behind the Scenes

*Because of my service dog, I was able to shift my focus away from the physical pain and the obstacles created by my **cerebral palsy**. I was given the freedom to pursue my personal goals and to spend more time and energy on the good things in my life.*

—Leigh Singh, from her essay
"Something Good"

A Touch of Humor

Joan Froling, one of the founders of the International Association of Assistance Dog Partners, tells a favorite story about her service dog, a Samoyed named Dakota. She taught Dakota to bring her a can of soda from the cupboard on command. When the dog delivered the can, she always rewarded it with a dog biscuit. One day, after crunching its reward, Dakota rushed off to the cupboard and brought back another can of soda, unasked. Froling gave it a fresh biscuit, and it dashed off for yet another can. Dakota had discovered a way to get unlimited dog biscuits from its human partner.

Libby, one of the first combination dog guide and assistance dogs, buys doughnuts for her owner.

Gleefully it went back and forth, emptying the cupboard, until Froling decided to stop giving rewards for cans she hadn't ordered.

As Froling points out, an assistance dog is never a mindless robot, or "push-button dog." "Actually," she says, "I'm afraid you'll discover an [assistance] dog is going to be pushing your buttons every now and again." Anyone who has lived with an assistance dog has stories of canine quirks, startling bits of dog logic, and embarrassing moments rescued by laughter.

Despite their intensive training, assistance dogs are not above getting into mischief. One woman fell asleep on a long plane flight, her dog guide curled up at her feet in the place usually reserved for carry-on bags. While its owner slept, the dog nosed its way into a bag under the seat in front of it and raided a box of cookies. When the unsuspecting passenger in the forward seat reached down for a snack, she encountered a cold nose. She let out a shriek that brought the flight attendants scurrying.

Another dog-guide partner sat in the front row of a little theater during a play. In a violent fight scene one of the actors fell dead at the edge of the stage. The dog guide, distressed by

What's That Dog Doing, Anyway?

People have endless misconceptions about the work of assistance dogs. One day a little boy watched a service dog lift boxes from a supermarket shelf for its owner, who used a wheelchair. The boy turned to his younger brother and explained, "See, that dog helps the lady look for bargains."

the commotion, anxiously licked the actor's face. The actor managed to stay in character and didn't move a muscle. The show must go on!

Heroic Moments

Sometimes an assistance dog helps in a way that goes far beyond the tasks it has learned by **rote**. By behaving intelligently in a crisis, assistance dogs have performed acts of true heroism.

Michael Patrick O'Shannon, an accountant, obtained a service dog shortly after a car accident left him paralyzed from the neck down. Barney, a Belgian Malinois, helped O'Shannon open doors, turn appliances on and off, and transfer in and out of his wheelchair. One night O'Shannon became critically ill with bleeding ulcers. Barney brought him the cordless phone so he could call for help. It then went to the door and opened it for the astonished paramedics.

A New York woman reports a remarkable story about her dog guide, a German shepherd named Mitzi. Every day she and Mitzi took the subway to and from work. But one morning when the train roared into the station, Mitzi refused to get on. Annoyed, the woman let the train pull out and waited for the next one, which Mitzi boarded without a problem. Later the woman learned that a fire had broken out on the first train, and several passengers were injured. Had Mitzi smelled the first trace of smoke? How did she know to disobey her partner's command?

Honoring Heroes

Every year exceptional assistance dogs are honored with the Service Dog of the Year Award sponsored by the Delta Society Service Dog Resource Center of Renton, Washington.

50

Saying Good-Bye

Mike Moran and his guide dog, Pax, seemed to have been born for one another. Pax, a gregarious German shepherd, and Moran, a rehabilitation counselor and aspiring actor, formed an unstoppable duo. But after nine years of service Pax became seriously ill. Moran made the agonizing decision to have Pax **euthanized**, or put to sleep. A few months later Moran returned to The Seeing Eye to train with another dog. But at first Moran felt that the new dog, a German shepherd named Duke, would never measure up to Pax. Months passed before he learned to appreciate Duke's cleverness, reliability,

Many animal helpers have kept their owners safe and out of harm's way.

Retirement Pensions

Many people choose retirement for an assistance dog that is still healthy but is too old to work. Often the person keeps the retired dog as a pet after obtaining a new assistance dog. Others find the retired dog an adoptive home. A retired assistance dog makes a gentle, well-behaved pet. After years of loyal service these dogs finally have a chance to relax and live a happy dog's life.

and playfulness. He grew to love Duke just as much as he had loved Pax before him.

The average working life of an assistance dog—from the time it is teamed with a human partner until its death or retirement—is about eight years. Eventually anyone paired with an assistance dog must endure the pain of loss. Most training programs have a waiting list, so a person may have to manage for several months before obtaining a new dog. Though this waiting period can be a hardship, it is also a time to grieve for the lost dog and prepare to welcome a new one.

Like Mike Moran, many people miss their previous dog intensely, and have a hard time forming a new bond. Yet each dog is unique and wonderful in its own way. Each one is to be loved, remembered, and celebrated.

Timeline

1919	After World World I, the German government begins to train dogs as guides for blinded veterans.
1928	Morris Frank trains with his first dog guide, Buddy, in Switzerland.
1929	Morris Frank and Dorothy Harrison Eustis start a dog-guide training program in Nashville, Tennessee.
1931	The Nashville school reopens as The Seeing Eye in Morristown, New Jersey.
1935	All U.S. railroads agree to let dog guides ride in passenger cars with their owners.
1938	Leader Dogs for the Blind is established in Rochester, Michigan.
1975	Agnes McGrath trains six dogs to work with deaf people, sponsored by the Minnesota SPCA.
1979	Paws with a Cause begins training hearing and service dogs.
1990	The Americans with Disabilities Act ensures public access to people using service animals in the United States.
1993	The International Association of Assistance Dog Partners is founded at a meeting in St. Louis, Missouri.
2001	Dan Shaw, a blind farmer from Maine, teams with the world's first trained guide horse.

Glossary

Americans with Disabilities Act—federal legislation passed in 1990 that ensures equal access to disabled people, including those with service animals

assistance dog—any dog trained to perform specific tasks that help a person with a disability

cerebral palsy—condition caused by damage to the brain which may affect speech, movement, and/or coordination

clearance—sufficient space for a person to pass an obstacle without colliding

companion dog—a dog trained to provide comfort to people in hospitals or nursing homes

dog guide—a dog trained to guide a person who is blind

euthanize—to kill an injured or very sick animal in a relatively painless manner out of mercy

hearing dog—a dog trained to signal a deaf person in response to specific sounds

intelligent disobedience—a dog guide's ability to disobey a command that could put its human partner in danger

legislation—a law

rehabilitation—the process of training a disabled person to live independently and to enter the workforce

rote—memorized routine

therapy dog—a dog used to help patients undergoing psychotherapy

To Find Out More

Books

Arnold, Caroline. *A Guide Dog Puppy Grows Up*. San Diego: Harcourt Brace, 1991.

Moore, Eva. *Buddy, The First Seeing Eye Dog*. New York: Scholastic, 1996.

Ring, Elizabeth. *Assistance Dogs: In Special Service*. New Milford, CT: Millbrook, 1993.

Smith, Elizabeth. *A Guide Dog Goes to School: The Story of a Dog Trained to Lead the Blind*. New Milford, CT: Millbrook, 1993.

Organizations and Online Sites

Assistance Dogs International
http://www.assistance-dogs-intl.org
This online site offers information about assistance-dog training and legislation pertaining to access for assistance dogs around the world. The site also includes personal accounts by assistance-dog partners.

Canine Companions for Independence
P. O. Box 446
Santa Rosa, CA 95402-0446
http://www.caninecompanions.org
This organization trains hearing dogs and service dogs.

Dogs for the Deaf
http://www.dogsforthedeaf.org
This organization provides hearing dogs. Its online site gives information about training and canine health.

Guide Dogs for the Blind
P. O. Box 151200
San Rafael, CA 94915-1200
http://www.guidedogs.com
This California-based organization trains dog guides for people throughout the United States.

The Guide Horse Foundation
2729 Rocky Ford Road
Kittrell, NC 27544
http://www.guidehorse.com
Learn more about the guide horses from this non-profit organization.

Paws with a Cause
4646 South Division
Wayland, MI 49348
http://www.pawswithacause.org
Trains a wide variety of assistance dogs as well as companion and therapy dogs.

The Seeing Eye, Inc.
P. O. Box 375
Morristown, NJ 07963-0375
http://www.seeingeye.org
The Seeing Eye is the oldest dog-guide training school in the United States. The site includes a video about Seeing Eye history.

A Note on Sources

Many books have been invaluable in my research about service animals. Among the earliest personal accounts of training and living with a dog guide are *First Lady of The Seeing Eye* by Morris Frank with Blake Clark, *Keep Your Head Up, Mr. Putnam* by Peter Putnam, and *My Eyes Have a Cold Nose* by Hector Chevigny. Two charming memoirs of life with hearing dogs are *Chelsea: The Story of a Signal Dog* by Paul Ogden and *Sounds Like Skipper: The Story of Kerena Marchant and Her Hearing Dog Skipper* by Kerena Marchant. *Partners in Independence: A Success Story of Dogs and the Disabled* by Ed and Toni Eames provides a thorough overview of the assistance-dog movement.

I would like to extend my special thanks to Ed and Toni Eames for their generosity in sharing resources and their enthusiasm about this book project. I would also like to thank

Joan Froling for her firsthand descriptions of life with a service dog.

Finally, I take this opportunity to thank the men and women of The Seeing Eye, Inc., for their ceaseless dedication and hard work. They trained my three dog guides, each one of them unforgettable. My direct experience working with dog guides was invaluable in writing this book.

—*Deborah Kent*

Index

Numbers in *italics* indicate illustrations.

About the Author

Deborah Kent grew up in Little Falls, New Jersey, where she was the first blind student to attend the local public school. She received her B.A. in English from Oberlin College and a master's degree from Smith College School for Social Work. After completing her social work degree she obtained her first guide dog, a black Labrador named Dee. She has had two other guide dogs, both German shepherds—Yulie and Tara.

Ms. Kent worked for four years at the University Settlement House in New York City. She then moved to the town of San Miguel de Allende in Mexico, where she wrote her first young-adult novel, *Belonging*.

Ms. Kent is the author of more than a dozen young-adult novels, as well as numerous nonfiction titles for children. She lives in Chicago with her husband, children's author R. Conrad Stein, and their daughter Janna.